Photographs of Devon from above

Ben Suermondt

Copyright © 2018 Ben Suermondt
All rights reserved.
ISBN: 1722966416
ISBN-13: 9781722966416

ACKNOWLEDGMENTS

All photographs taken from a drone within accordance of the Drone code within the UK.

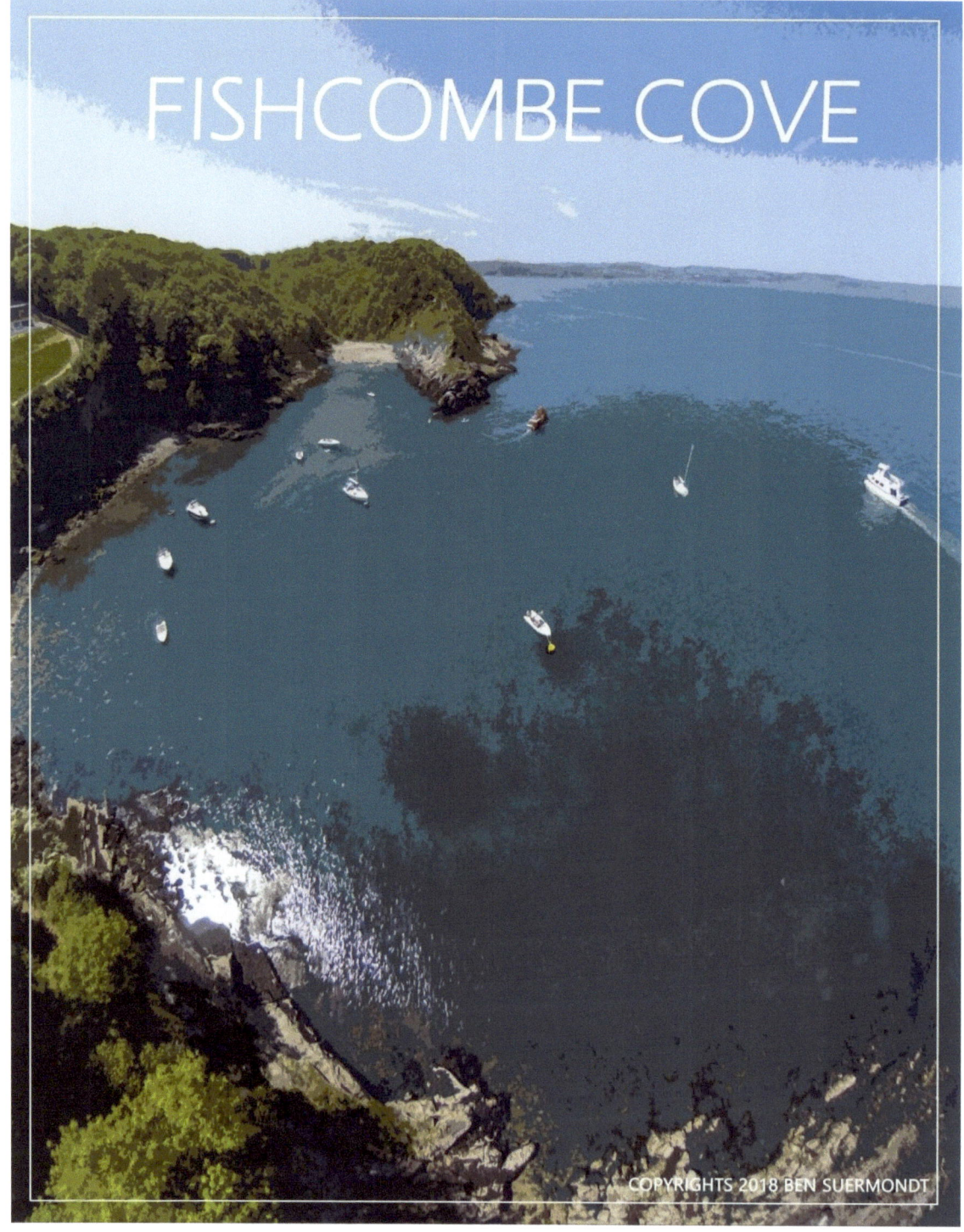

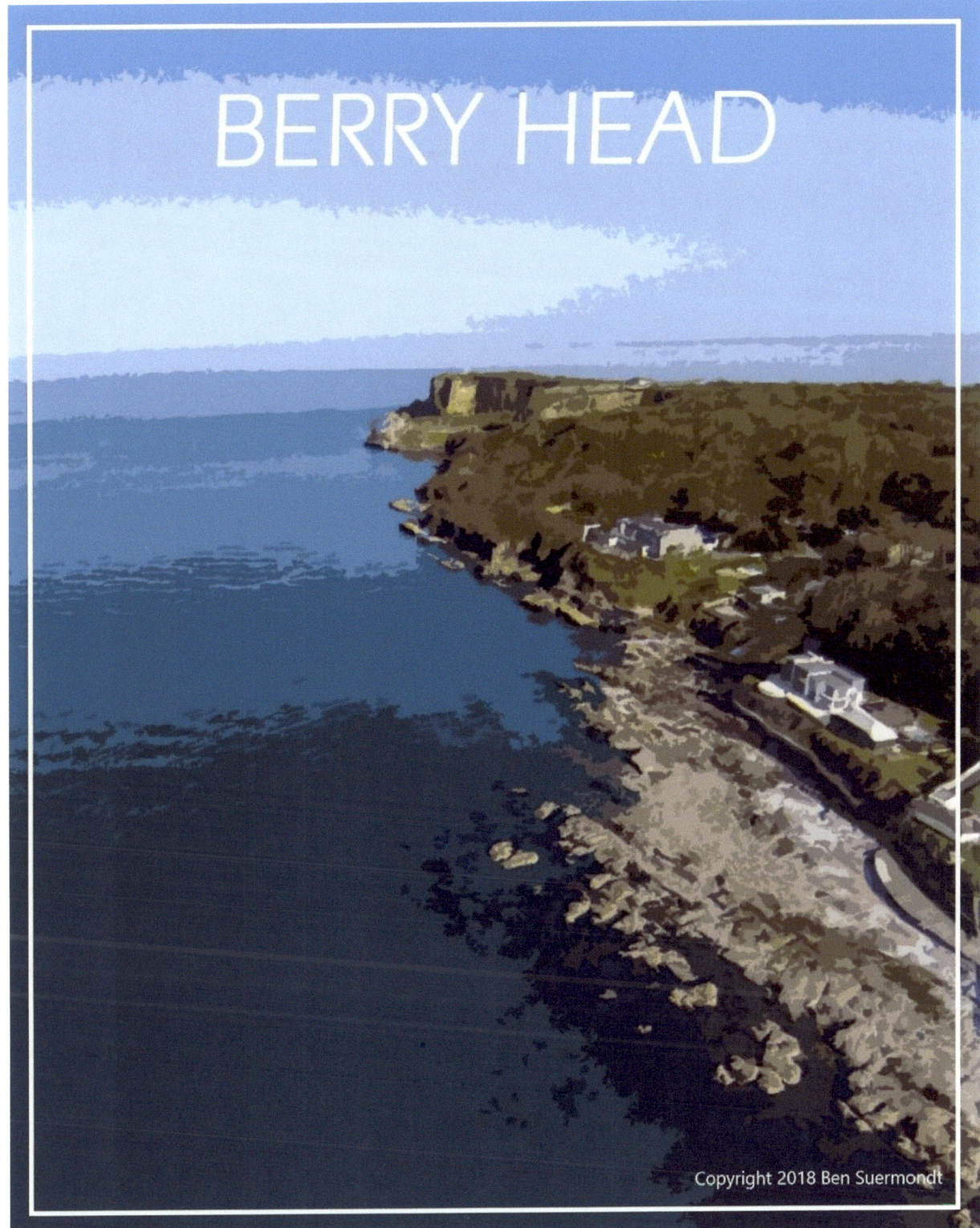

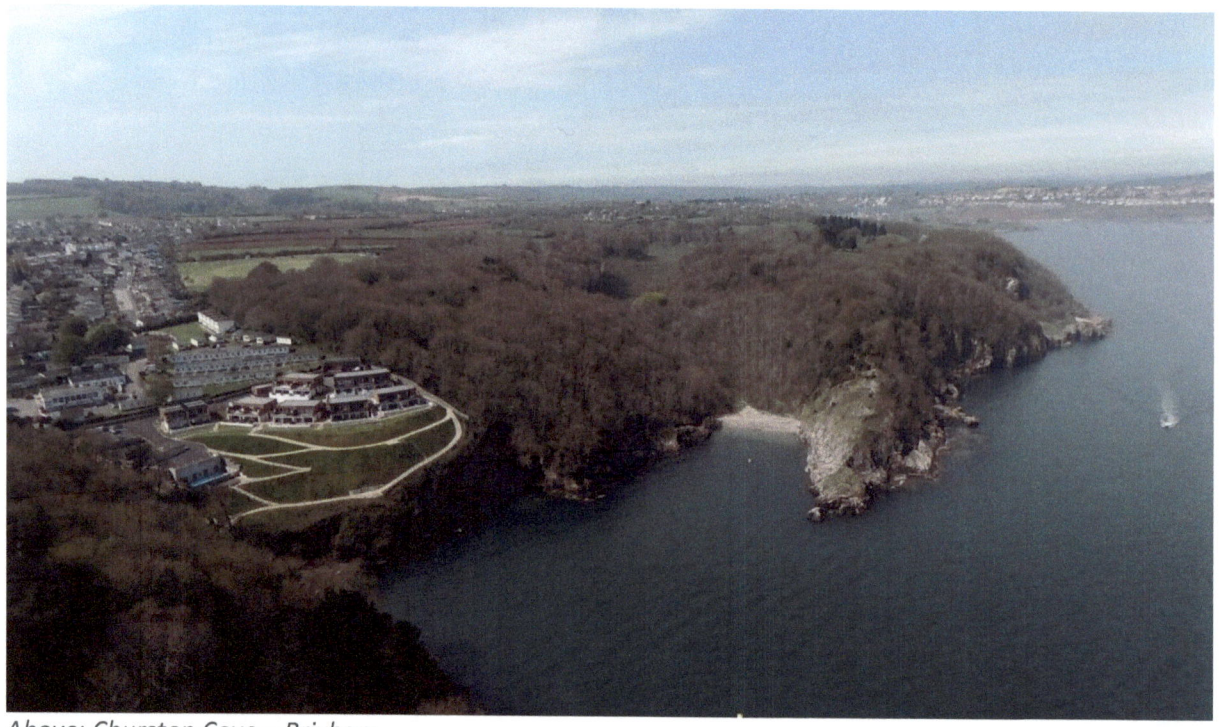
Above: Churston Cove – Brixham

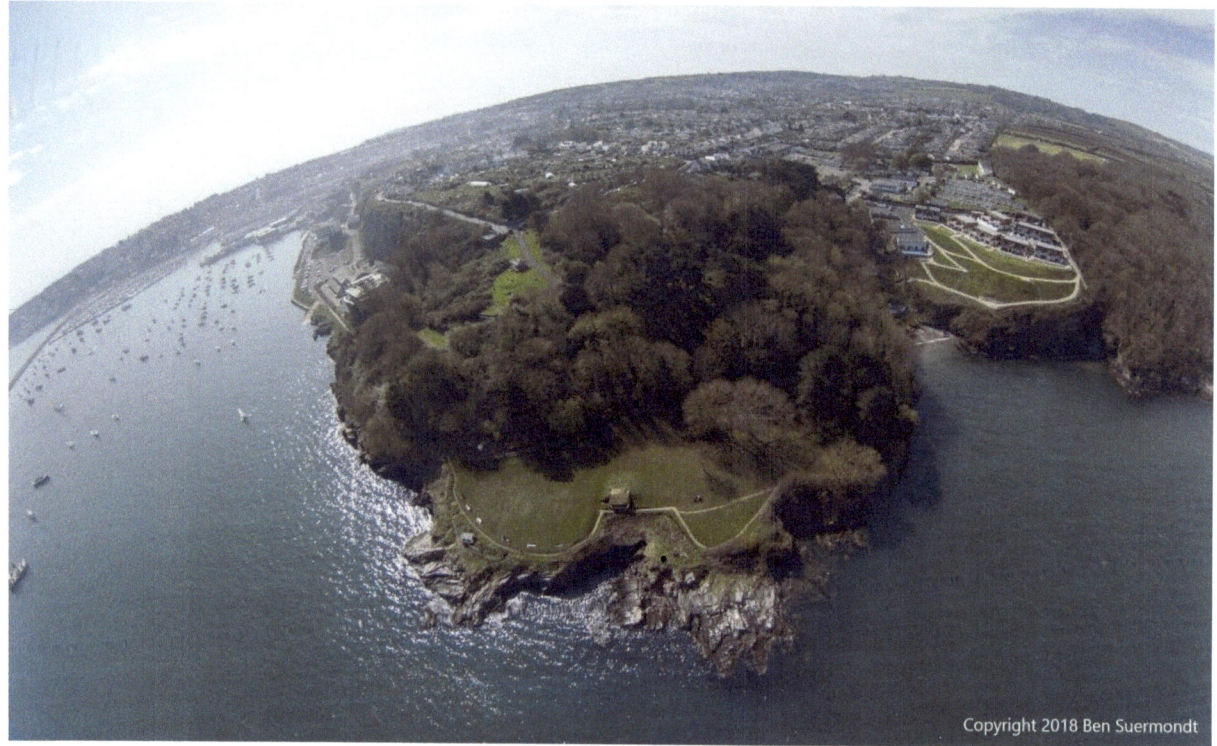
Above: Battery gardens headland and Fishcombe cove – Brixham

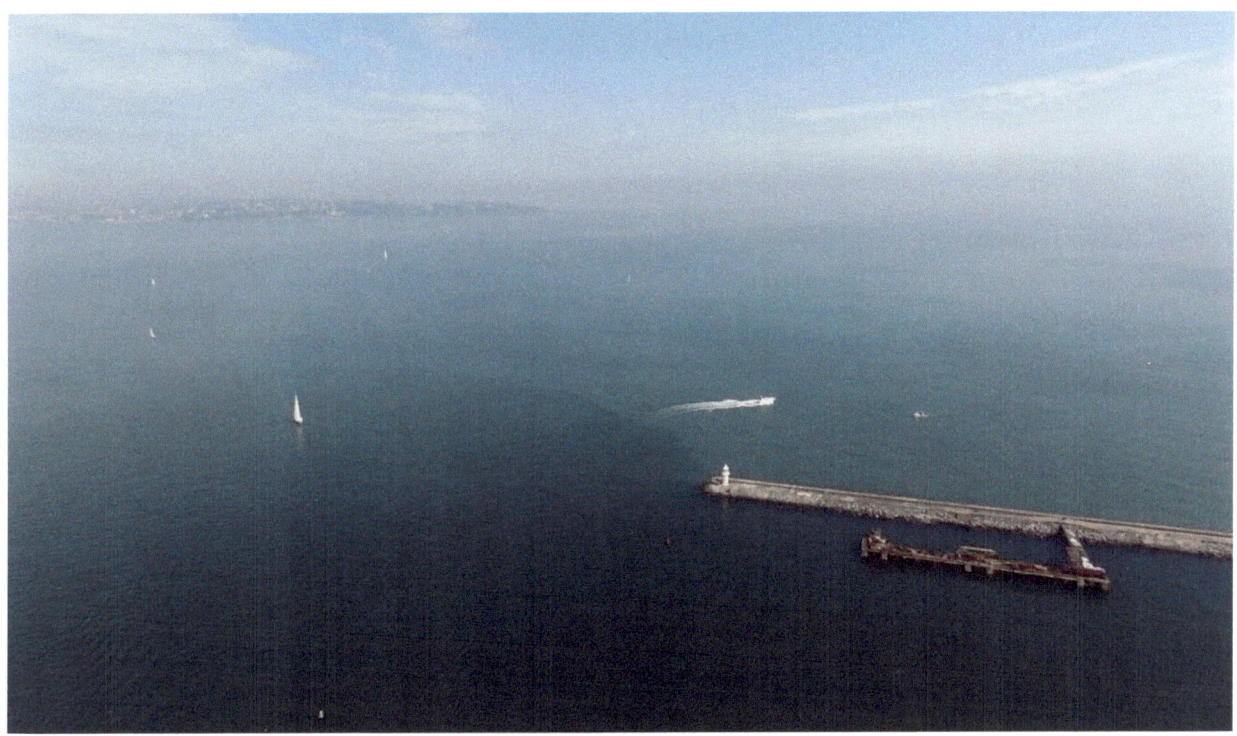
Above: Brixham breakwater looking out to sea – Brixham

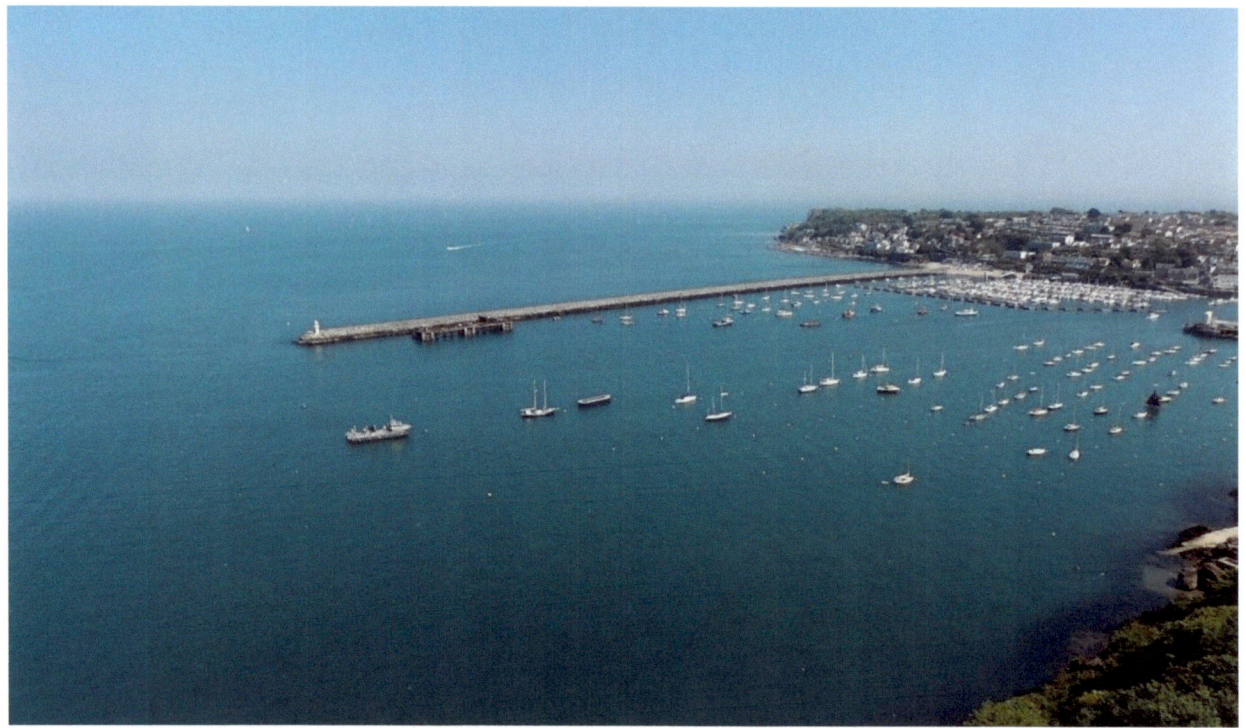
Above: Brixham outer harbour - Brixham

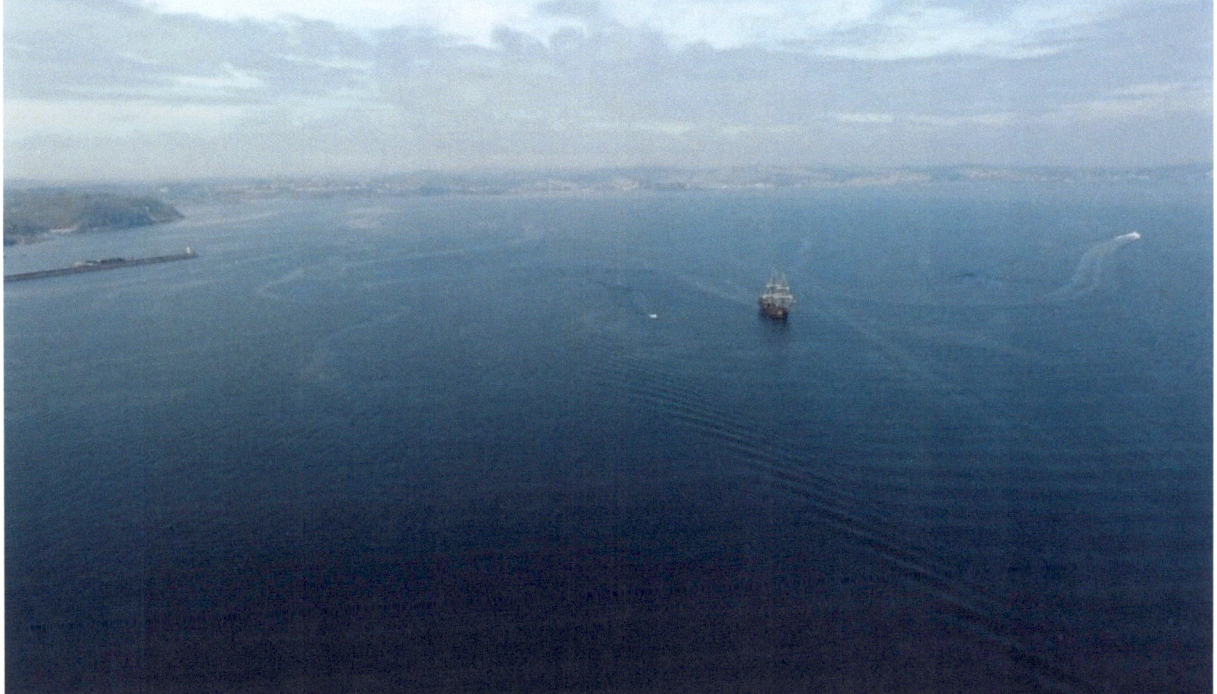
Above: The El Galleon leaving the port of Brixham

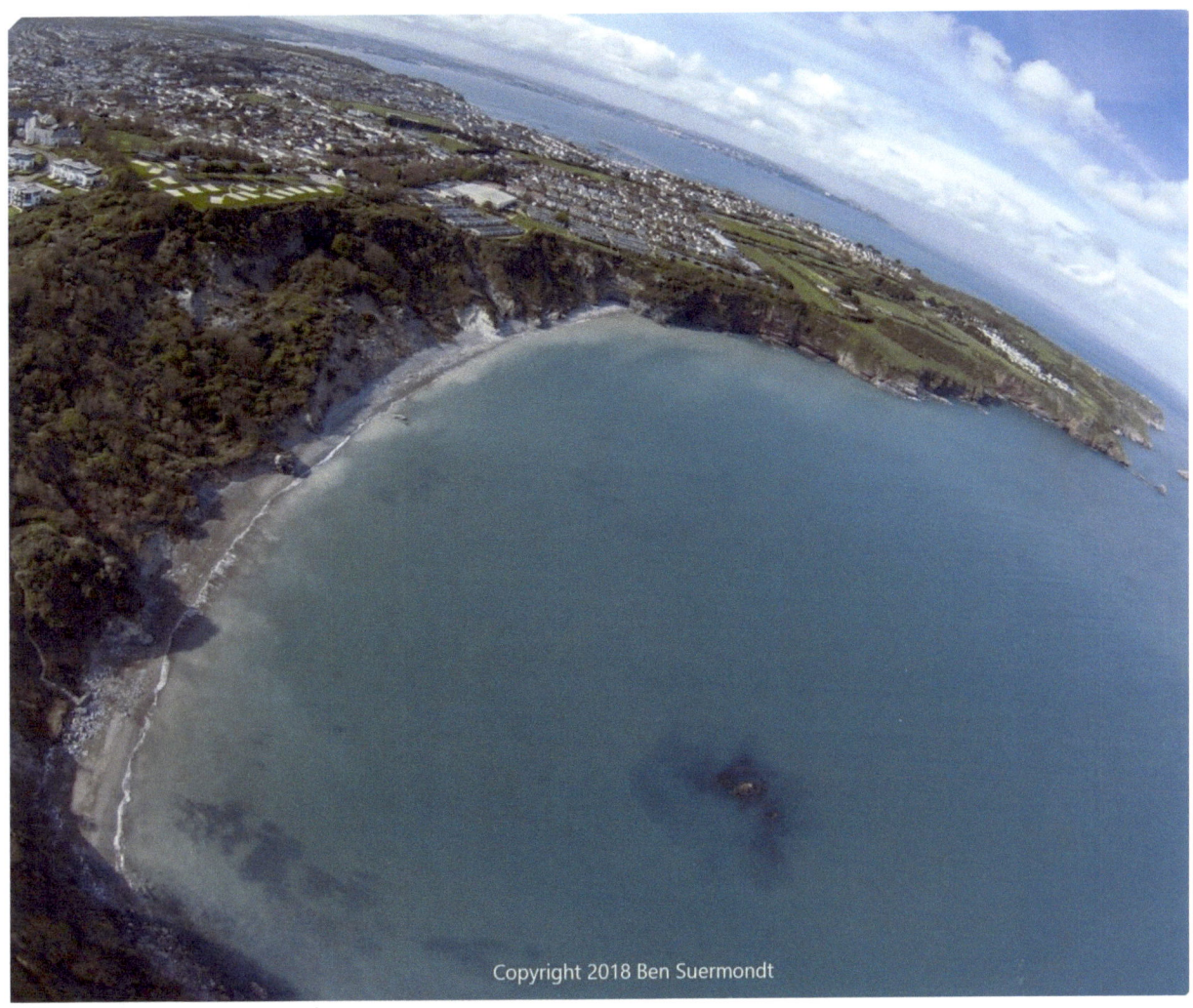
Above: St Marys Bay – Brixham

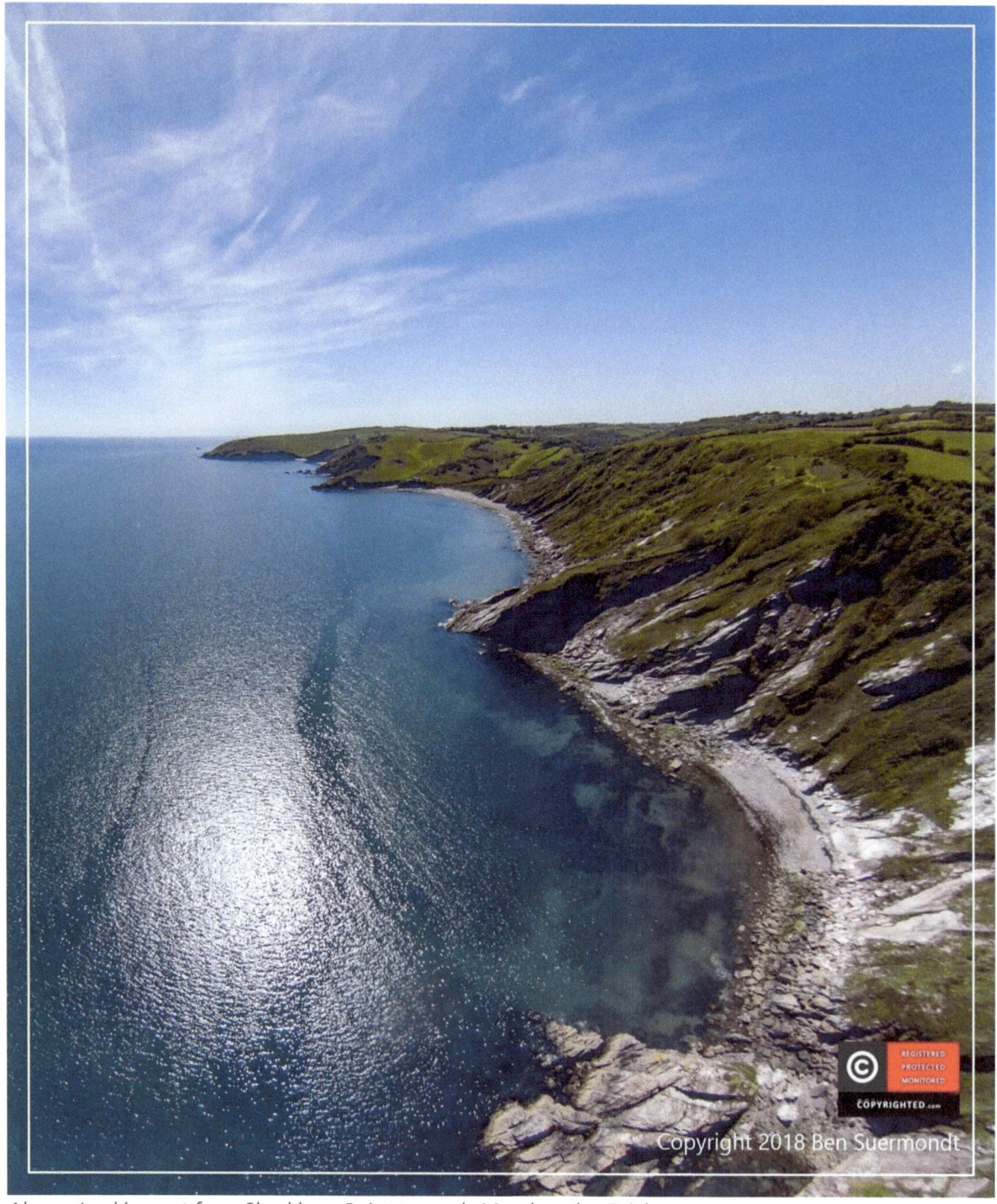

Above: Looking out from Sharkham Point towards Mandsands - Brixham

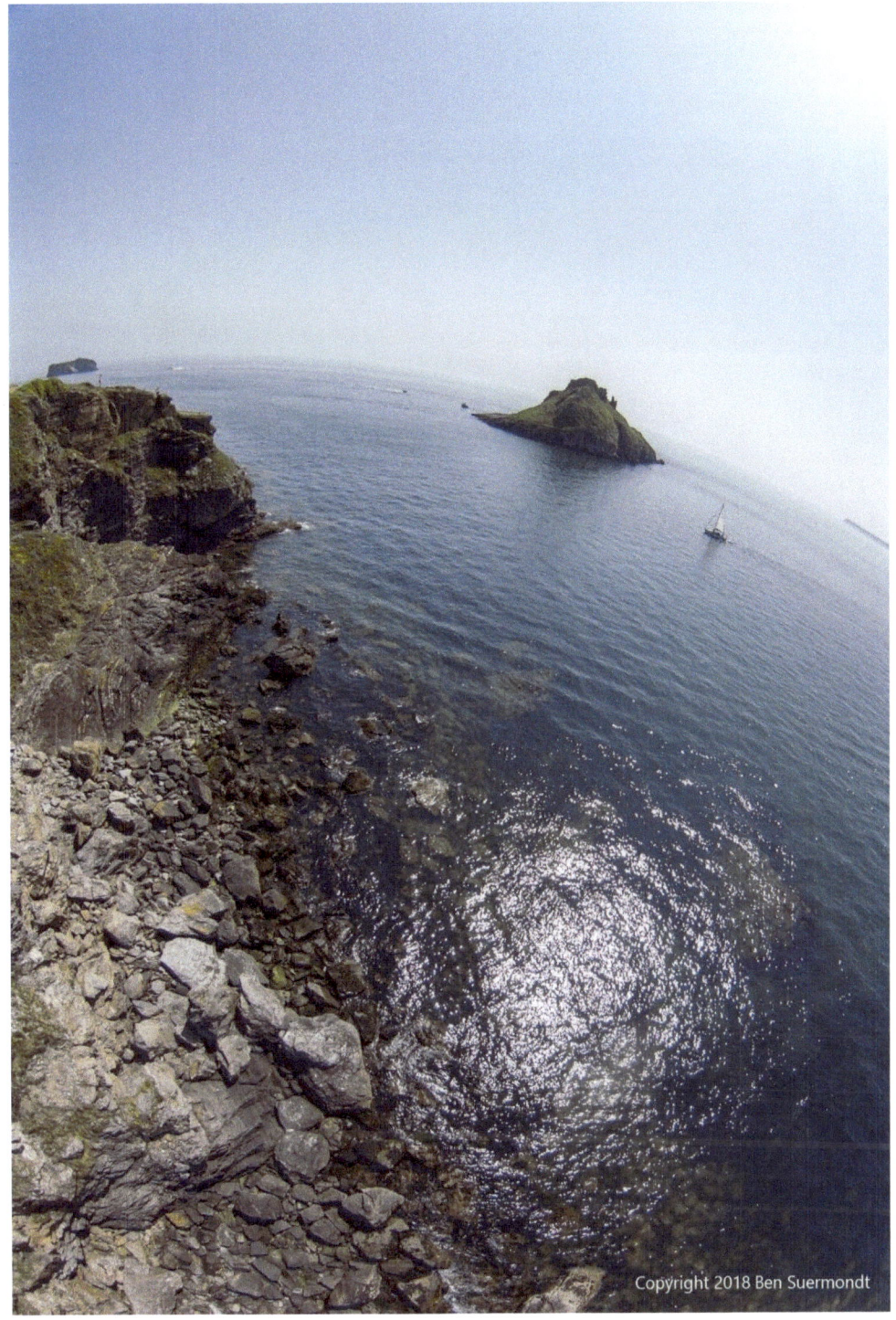

Above: Thatcher's Rock - Torquay

3 THE RIVER DART

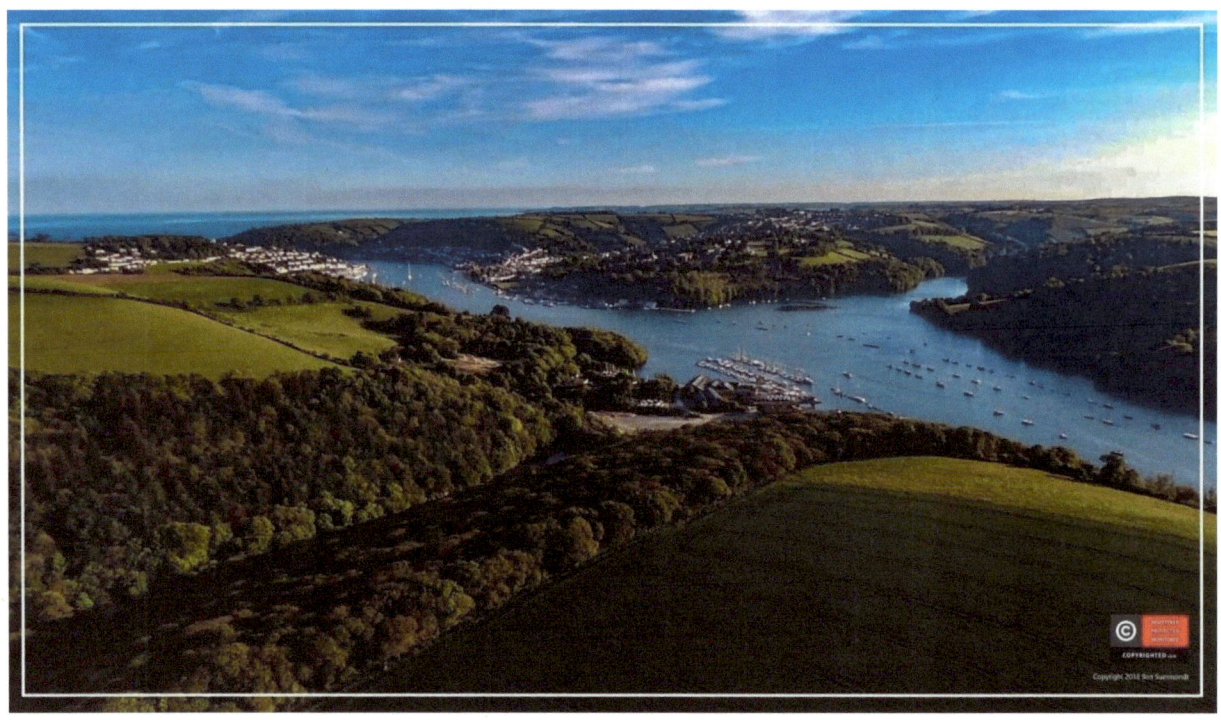

Above: Looking over the fields over Noss Mariner with Kingswear and Dartmouth in the background.

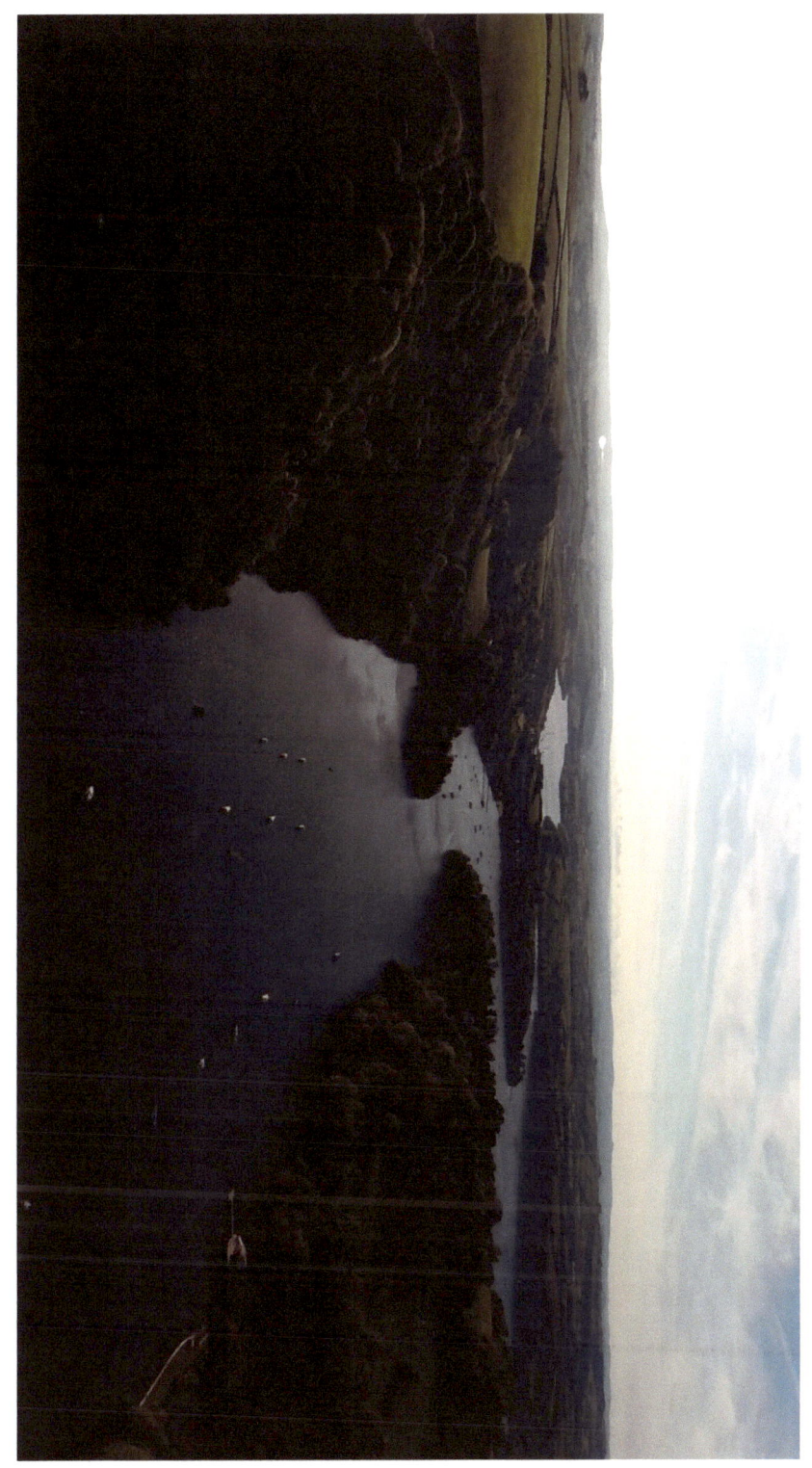

Above: The River Dart looking up the river towards Greenaway.

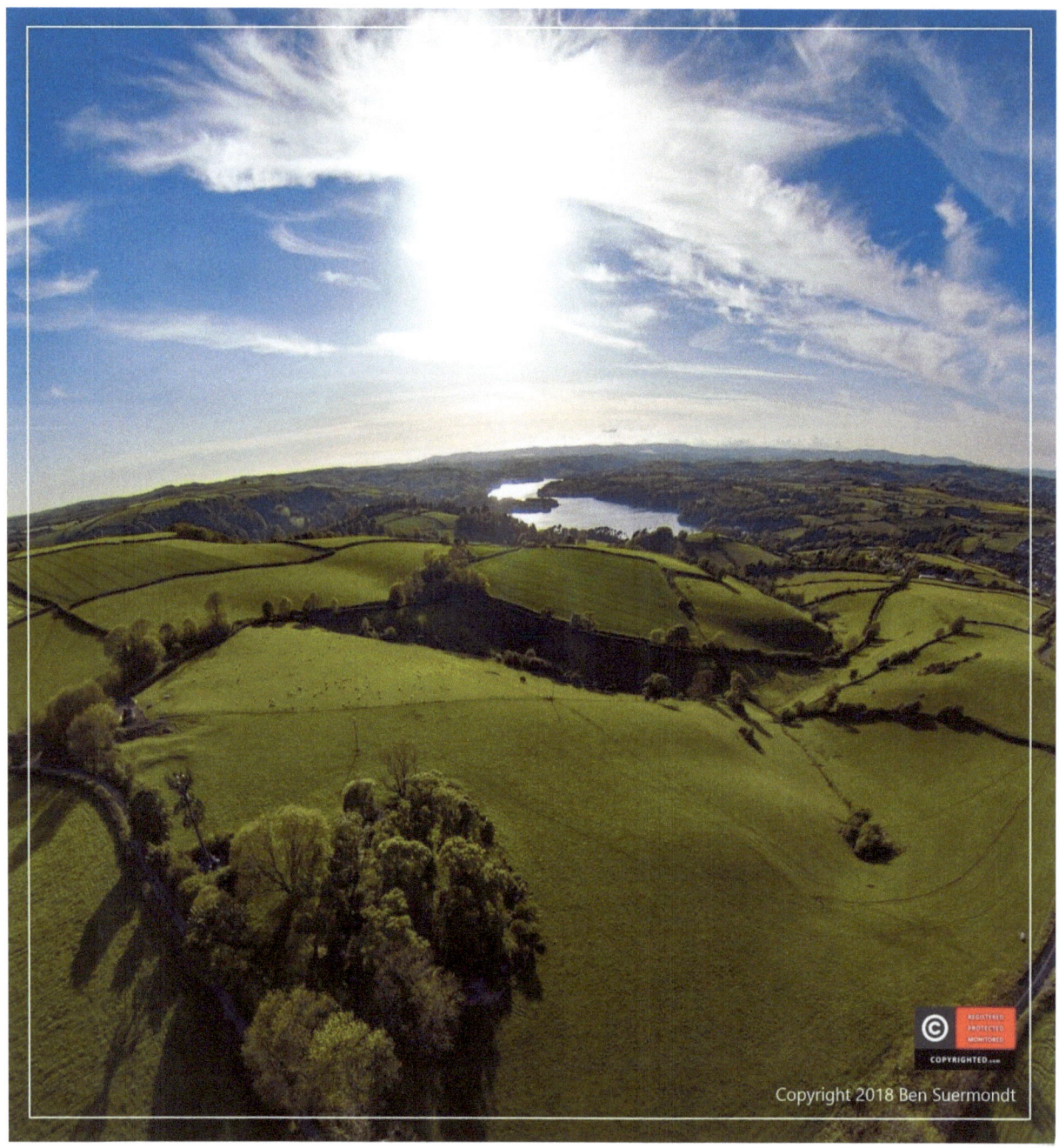

Above: Looking across the fields over Greenaway up the River Dart.

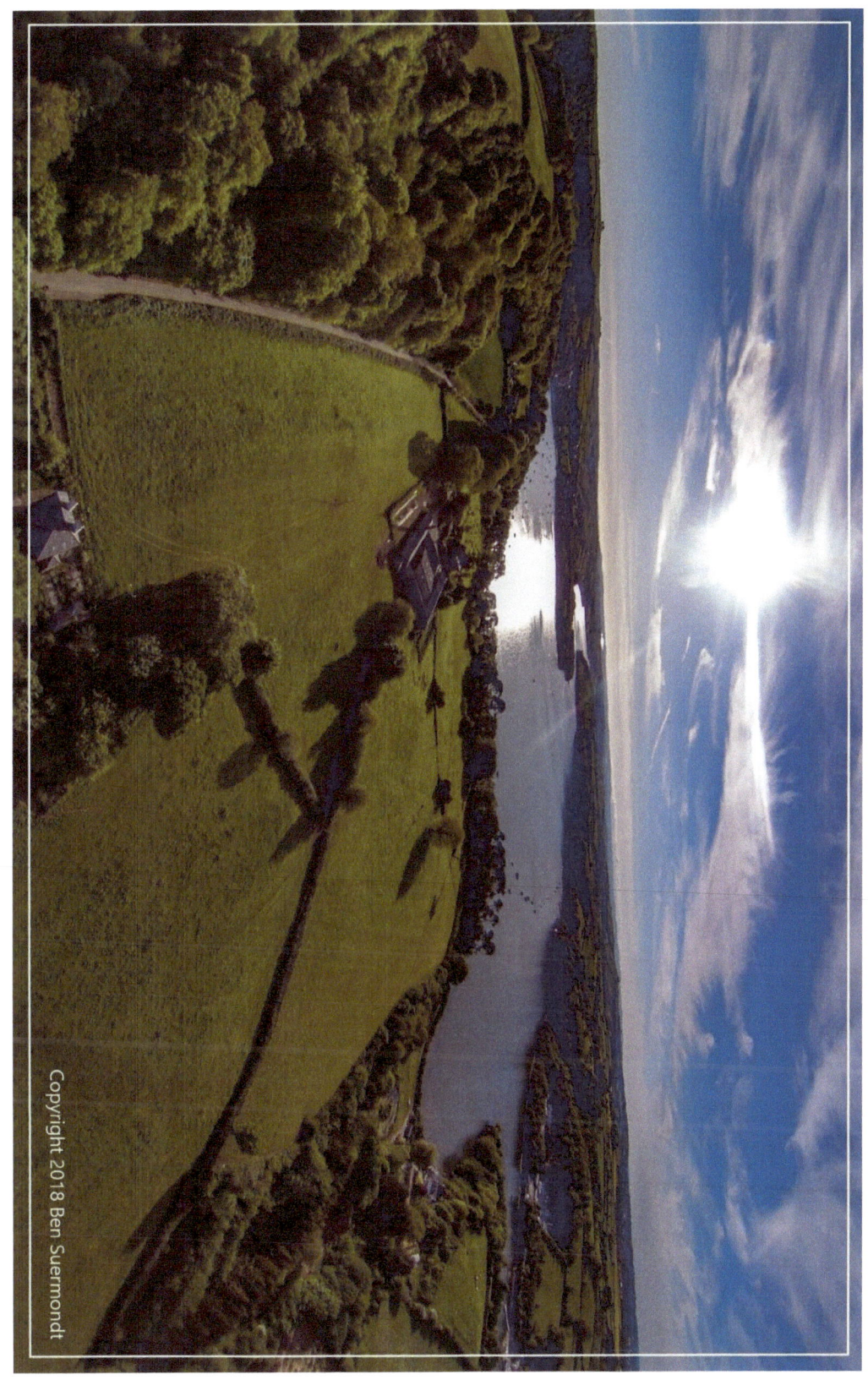

4 DARTMOOR

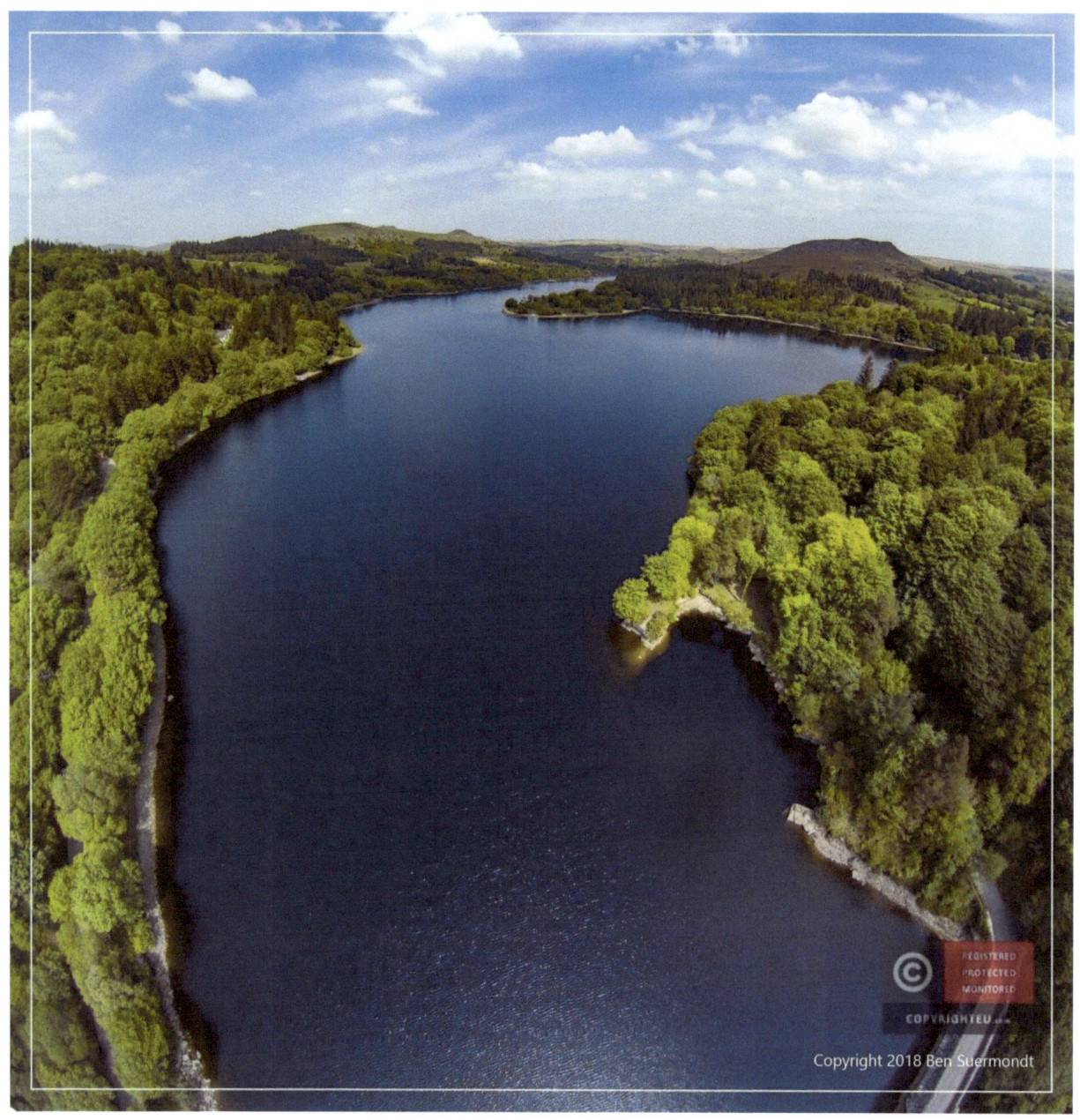

Above: Burrator Reservoir

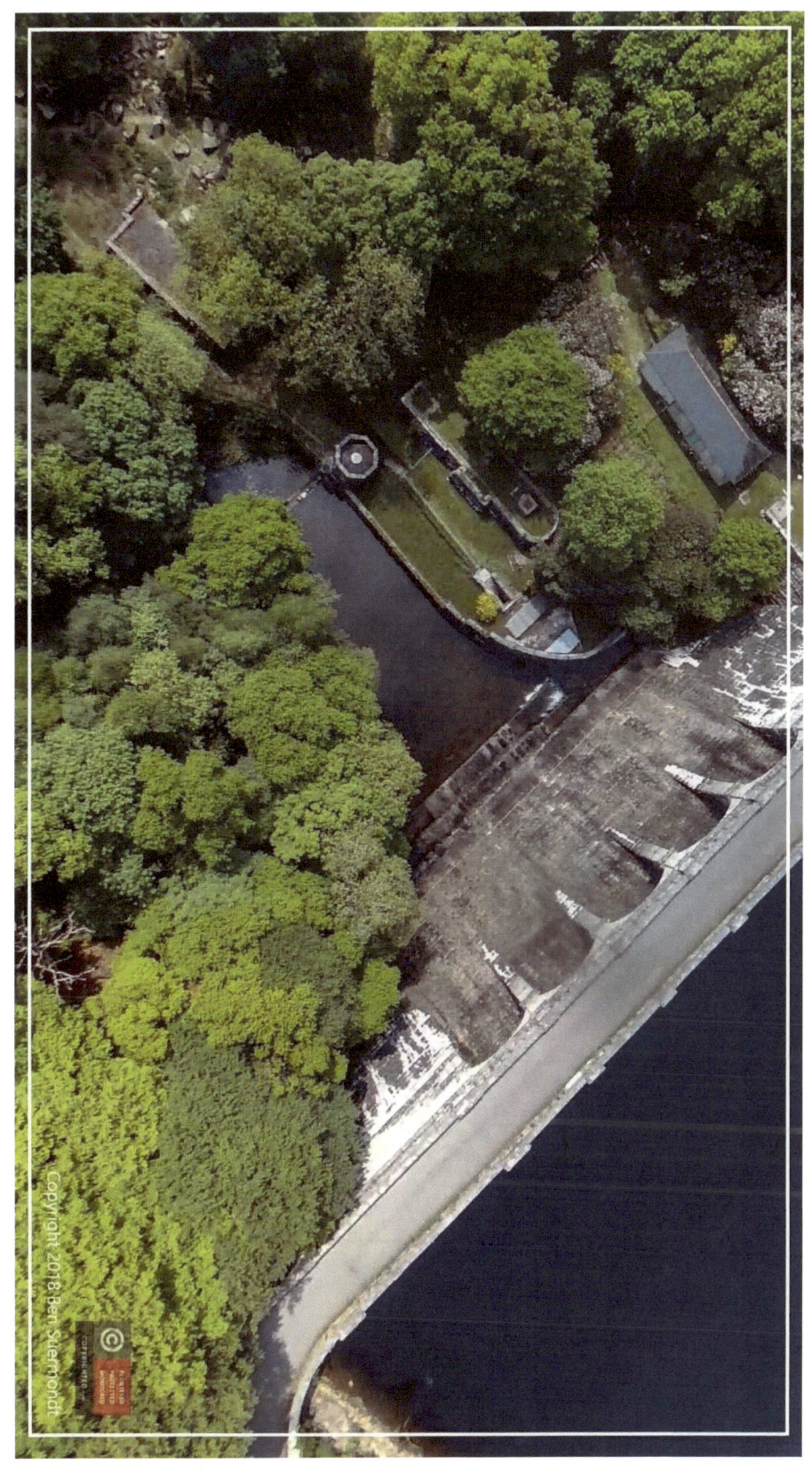

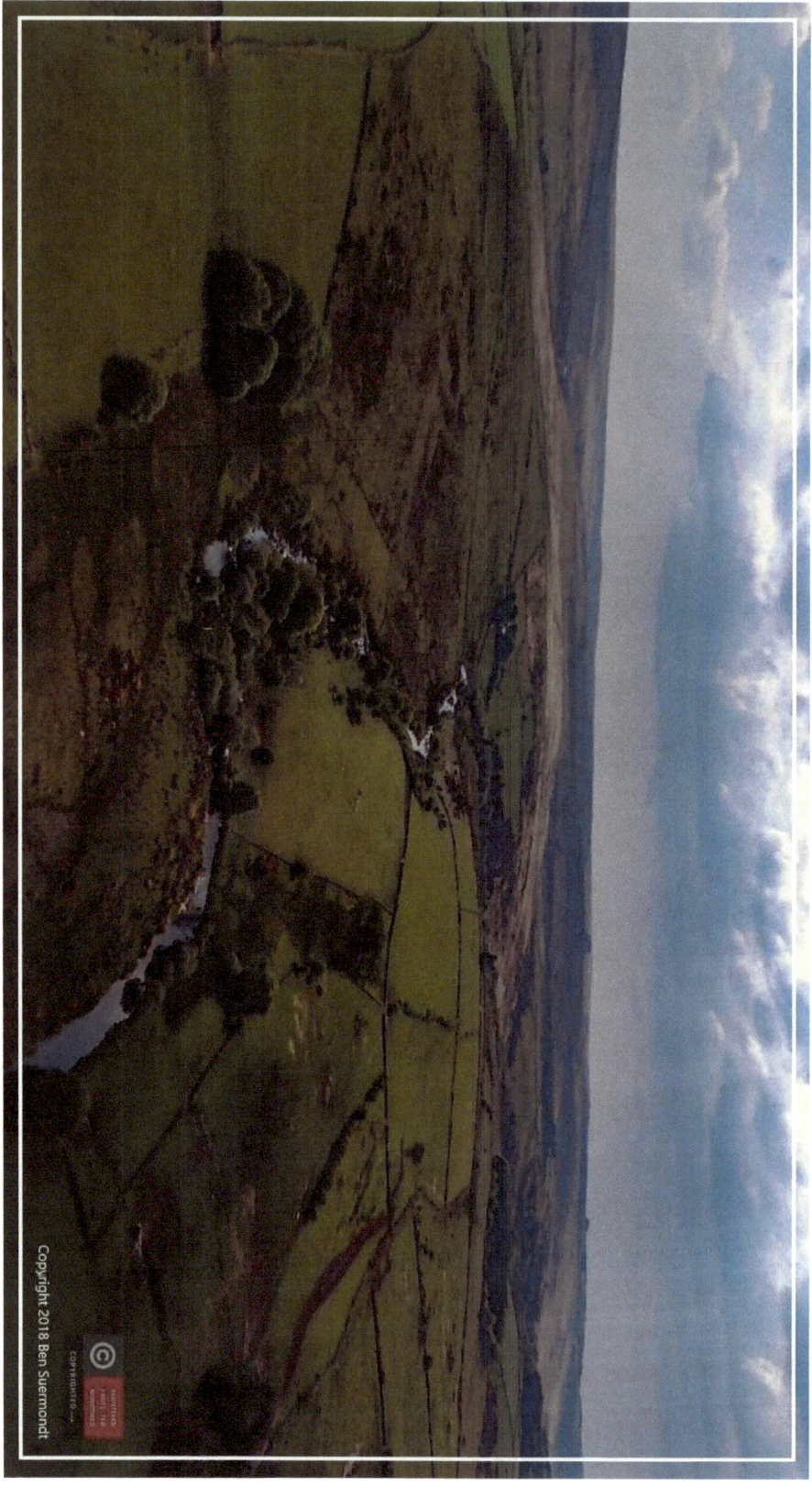

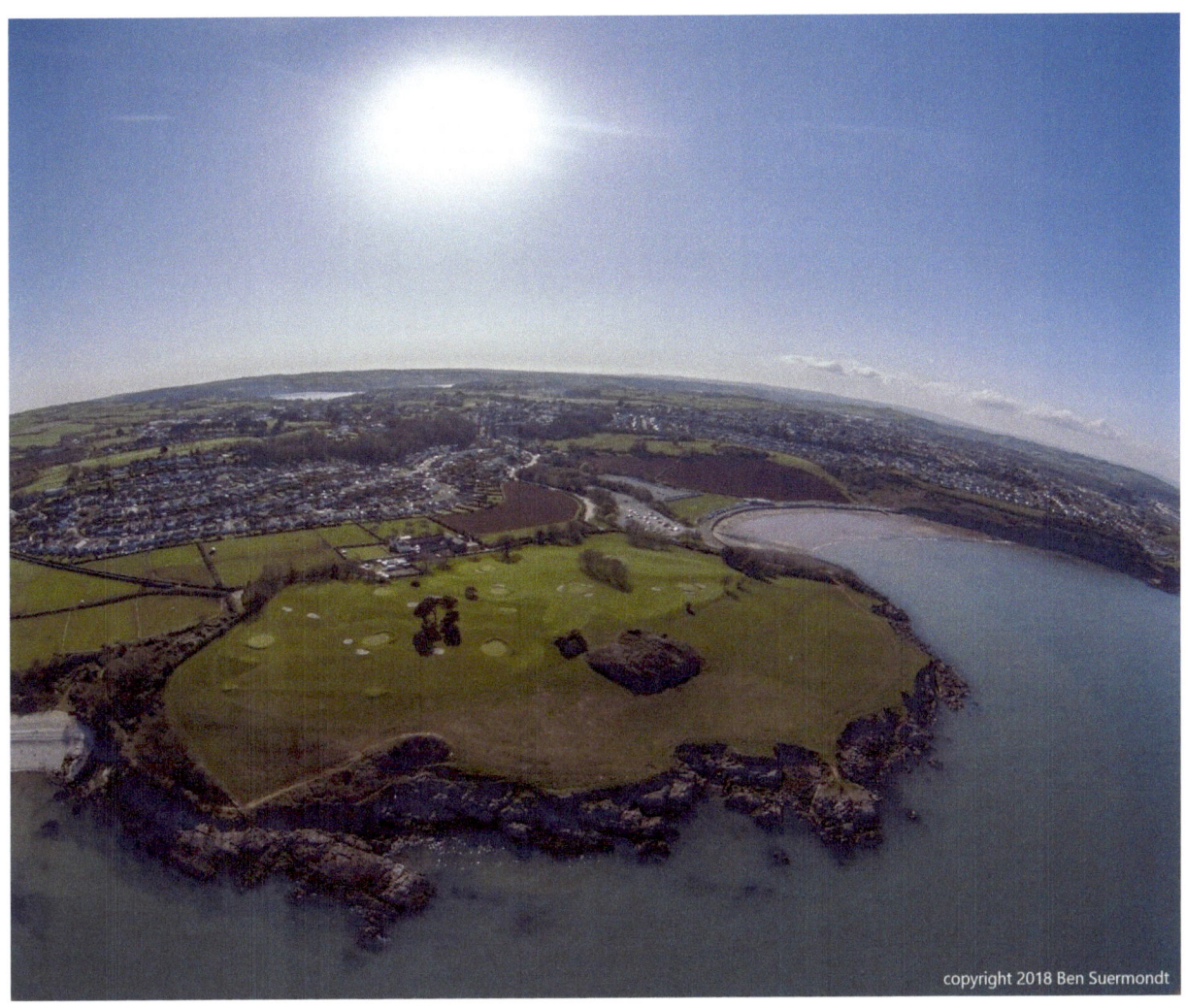

Above: Broad sands Headland - Brixham

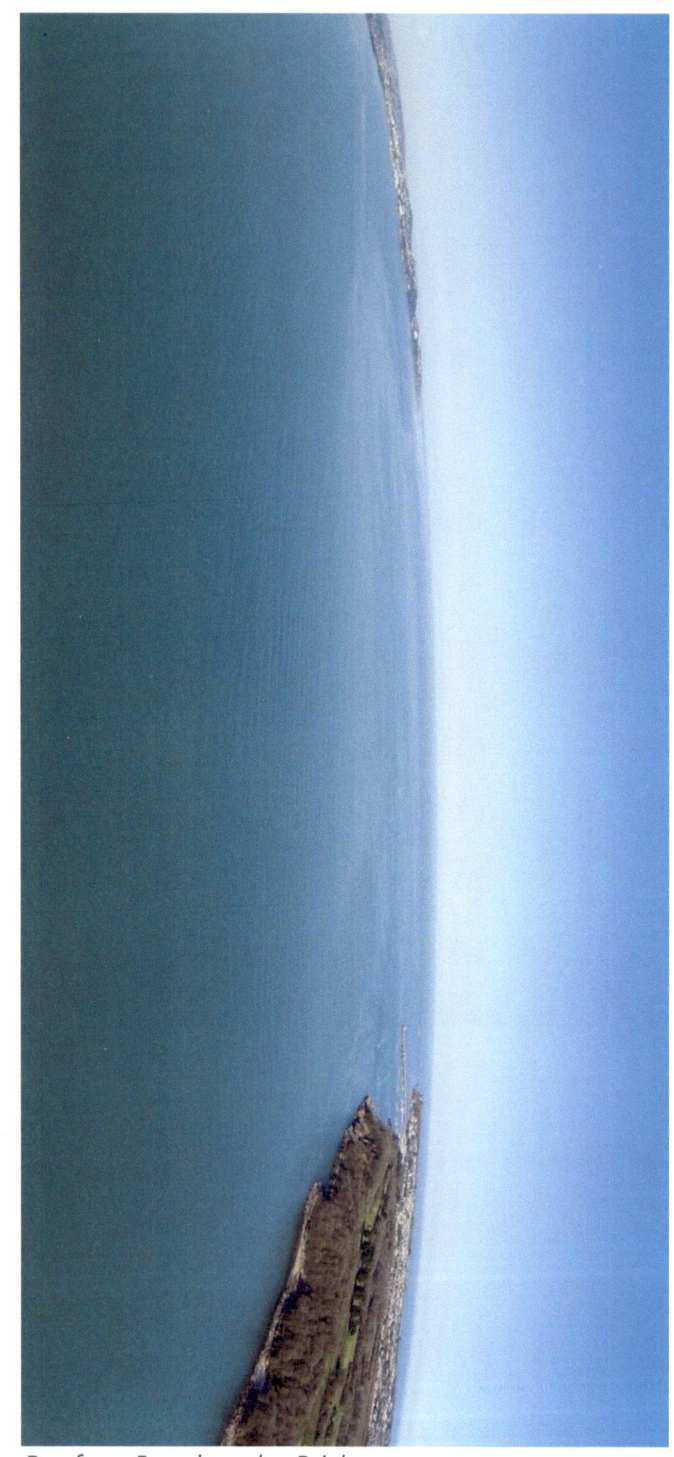

Above: Looking into The Bay from Broad sands - Brixham

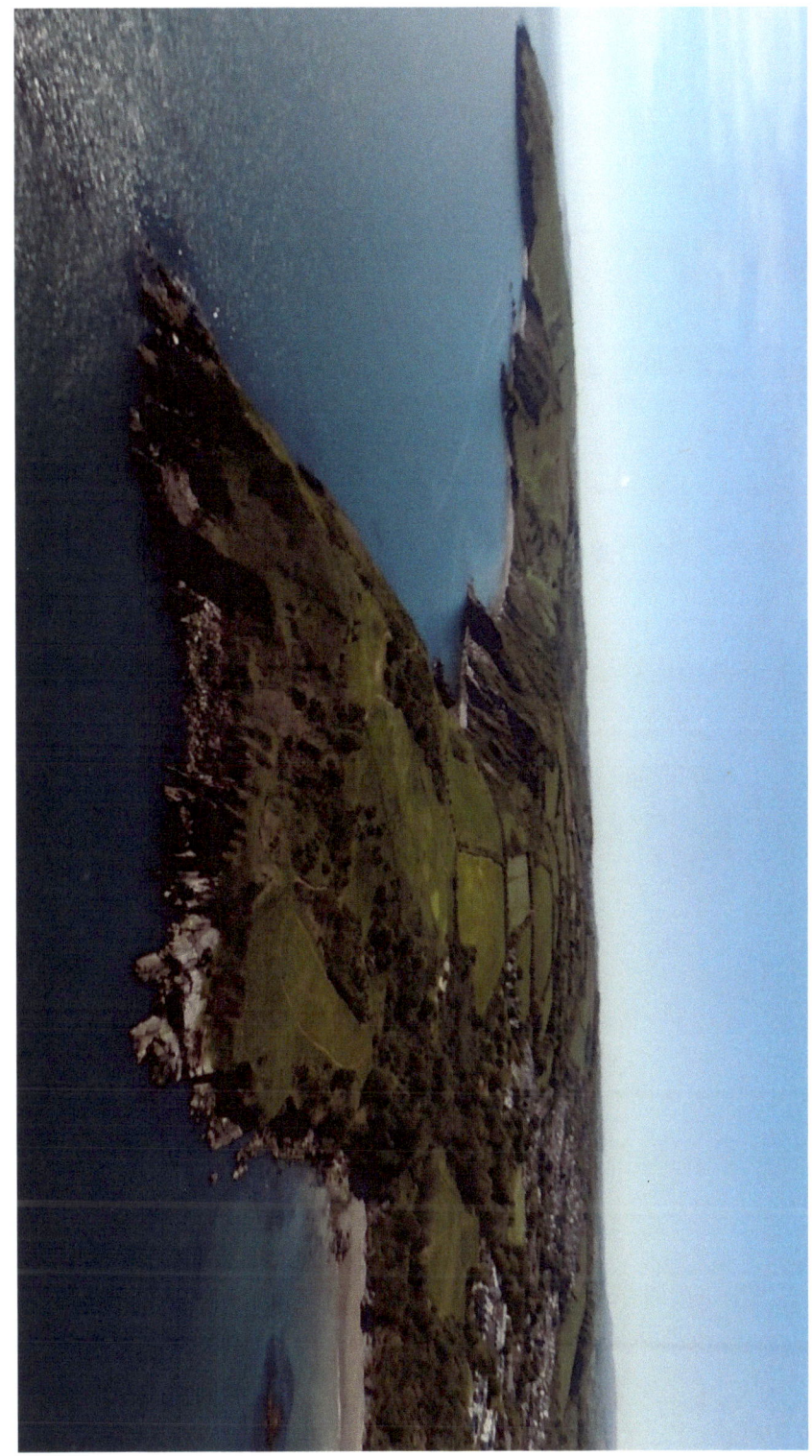

Above: Sharkham headland - Brixham

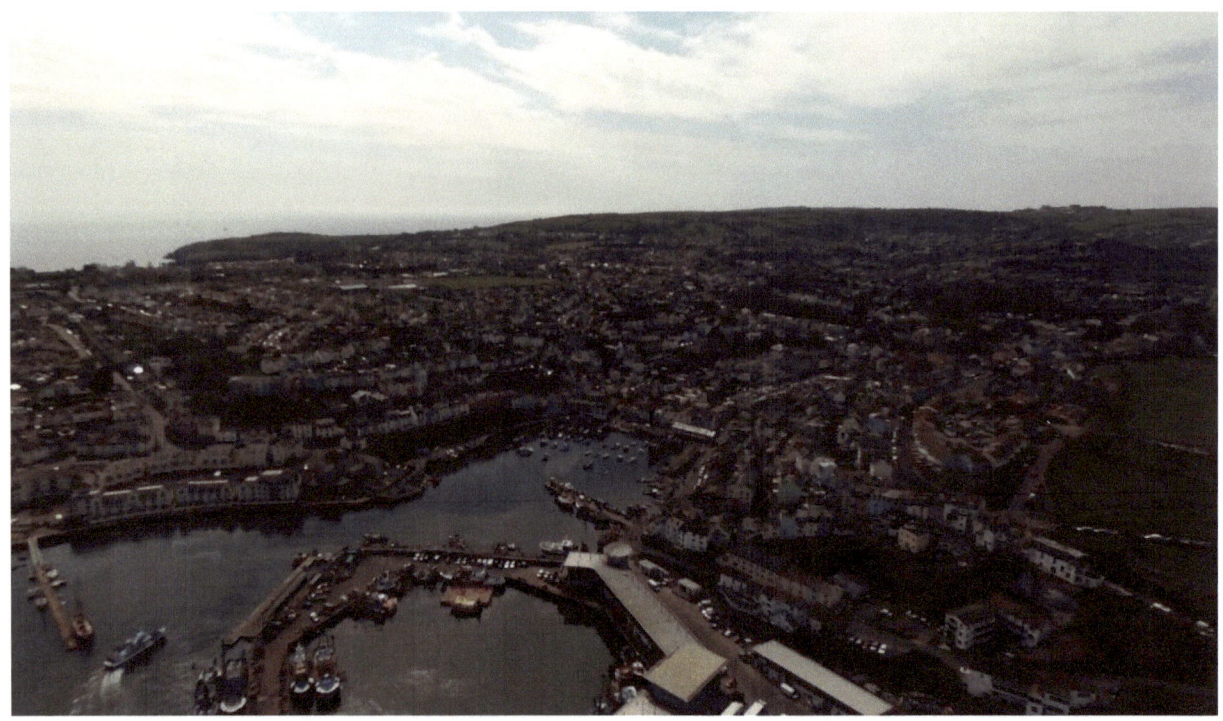

Above: Brixham inner harbour.
Below: Brixham Fishing Port.

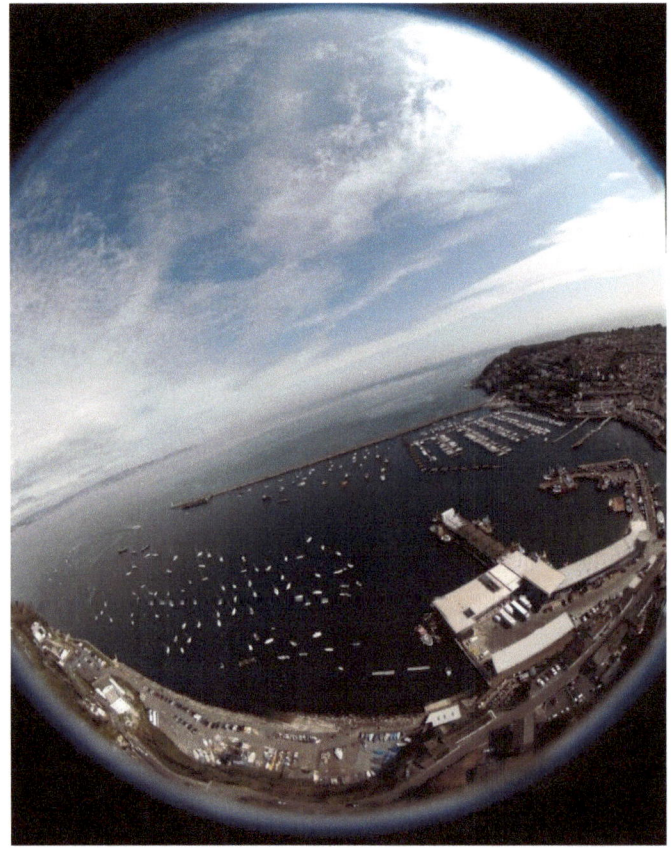

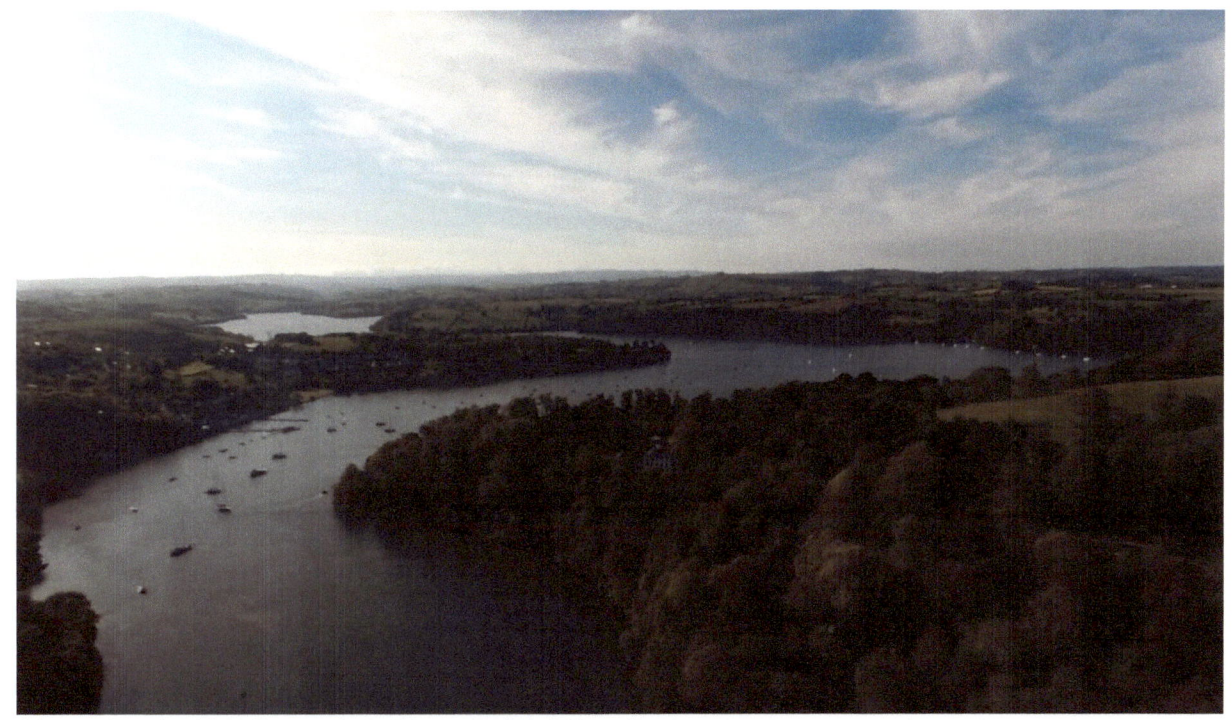

Above: Overlooking Greenaway Estate and the River Dart

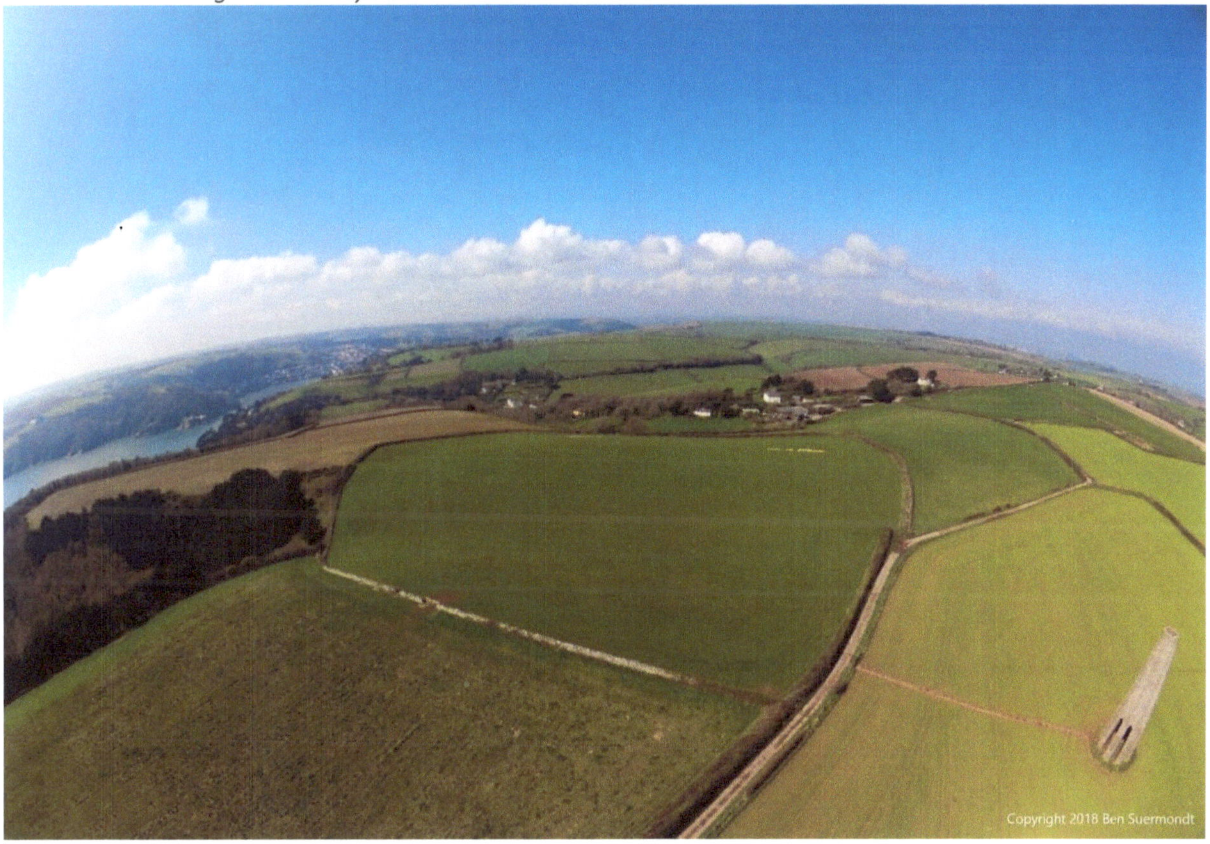

Above: Brownstone day marker - Kingswear

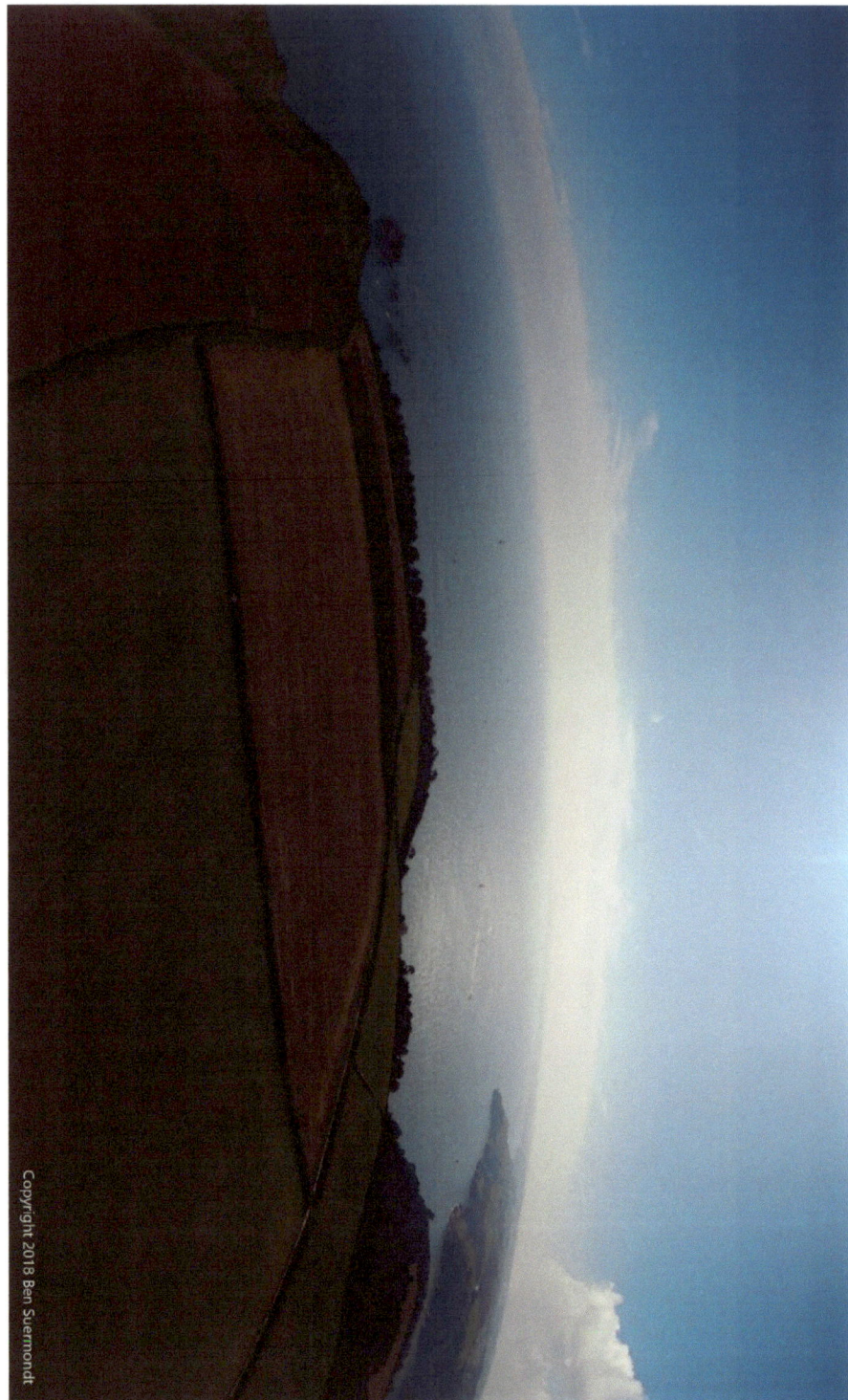
Above: Looking out across Start Bay from Brownstone – Kingswear

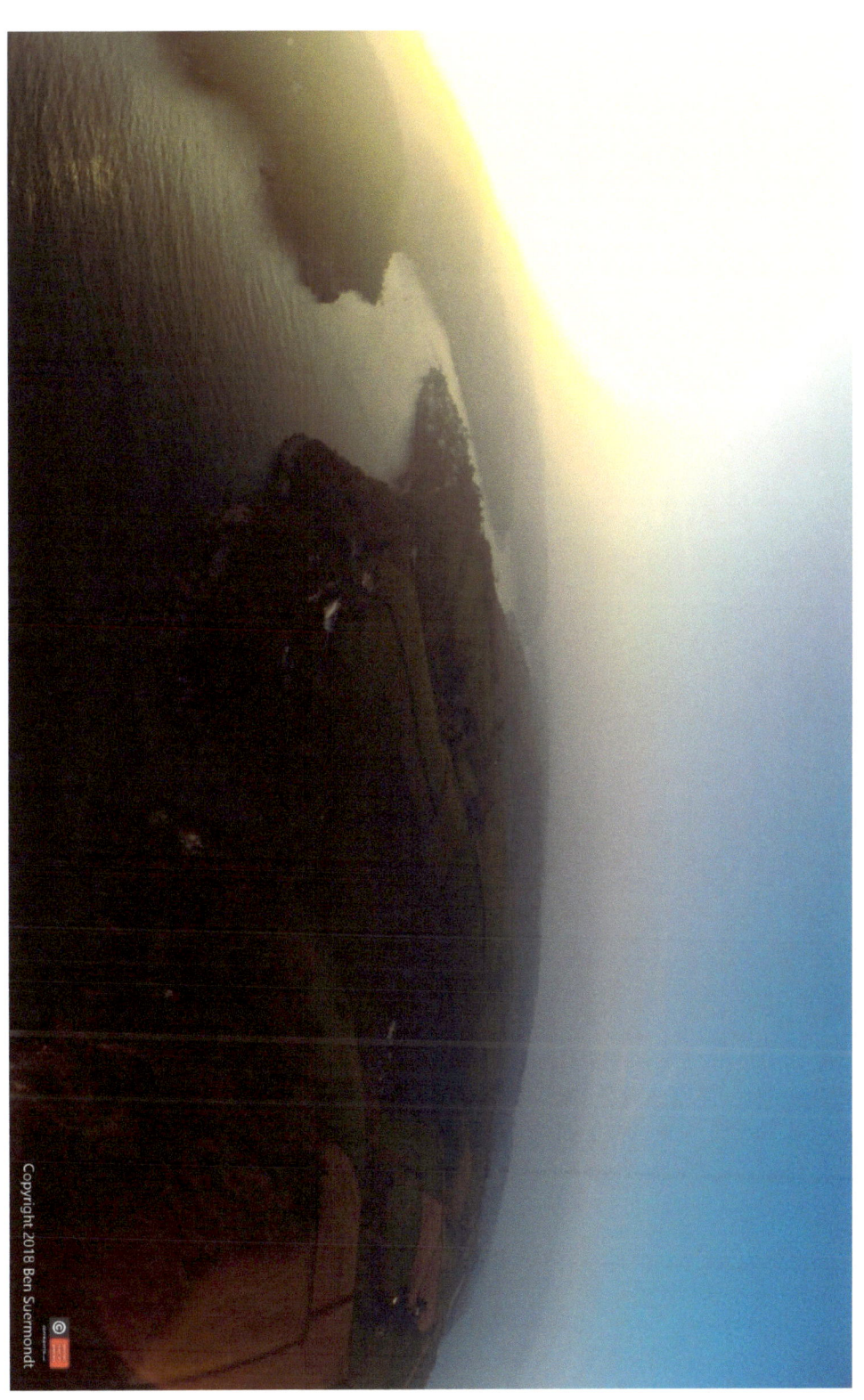

Left: The Mouth of The River Dart

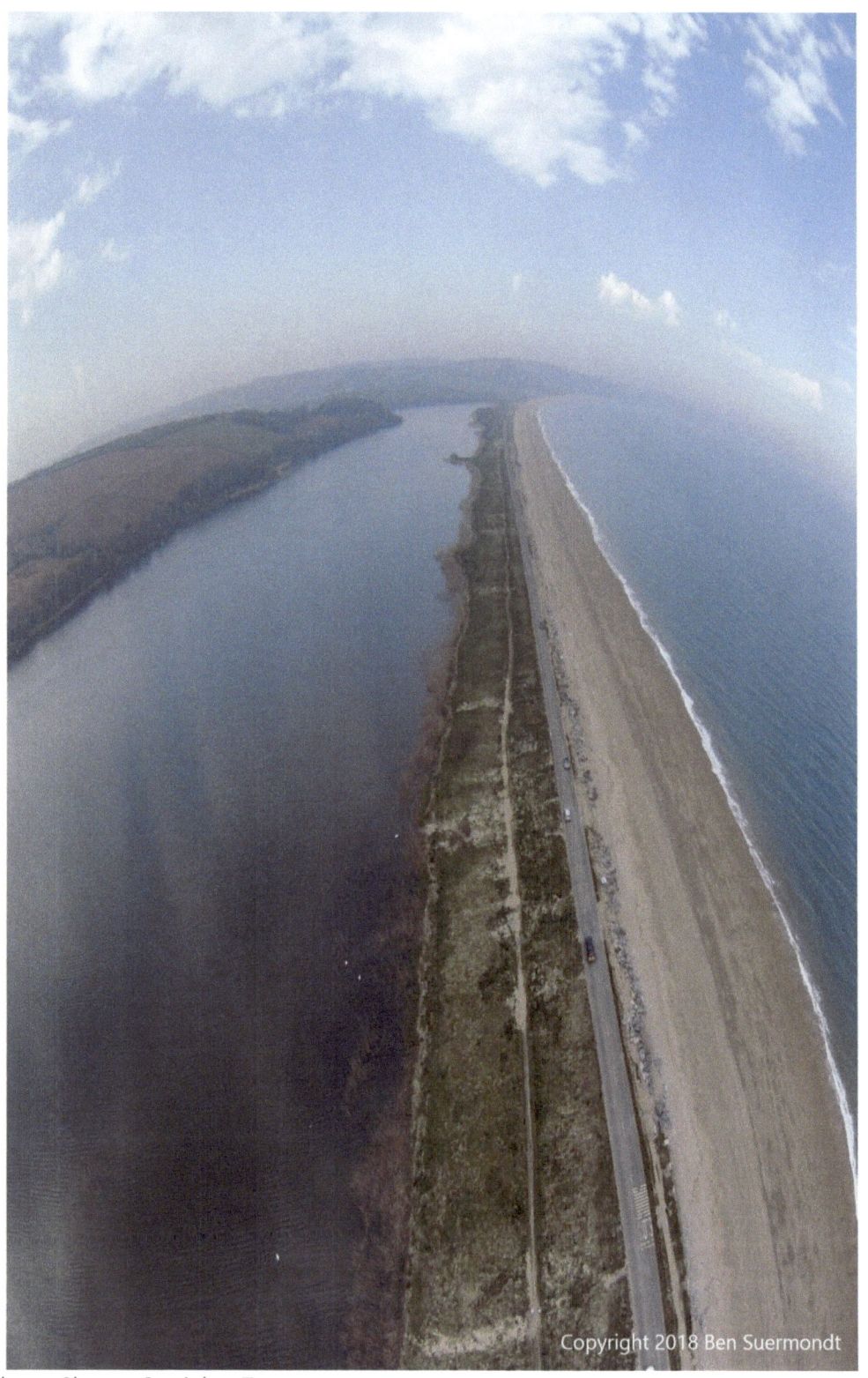

Above: Slapton Straight - Torcross

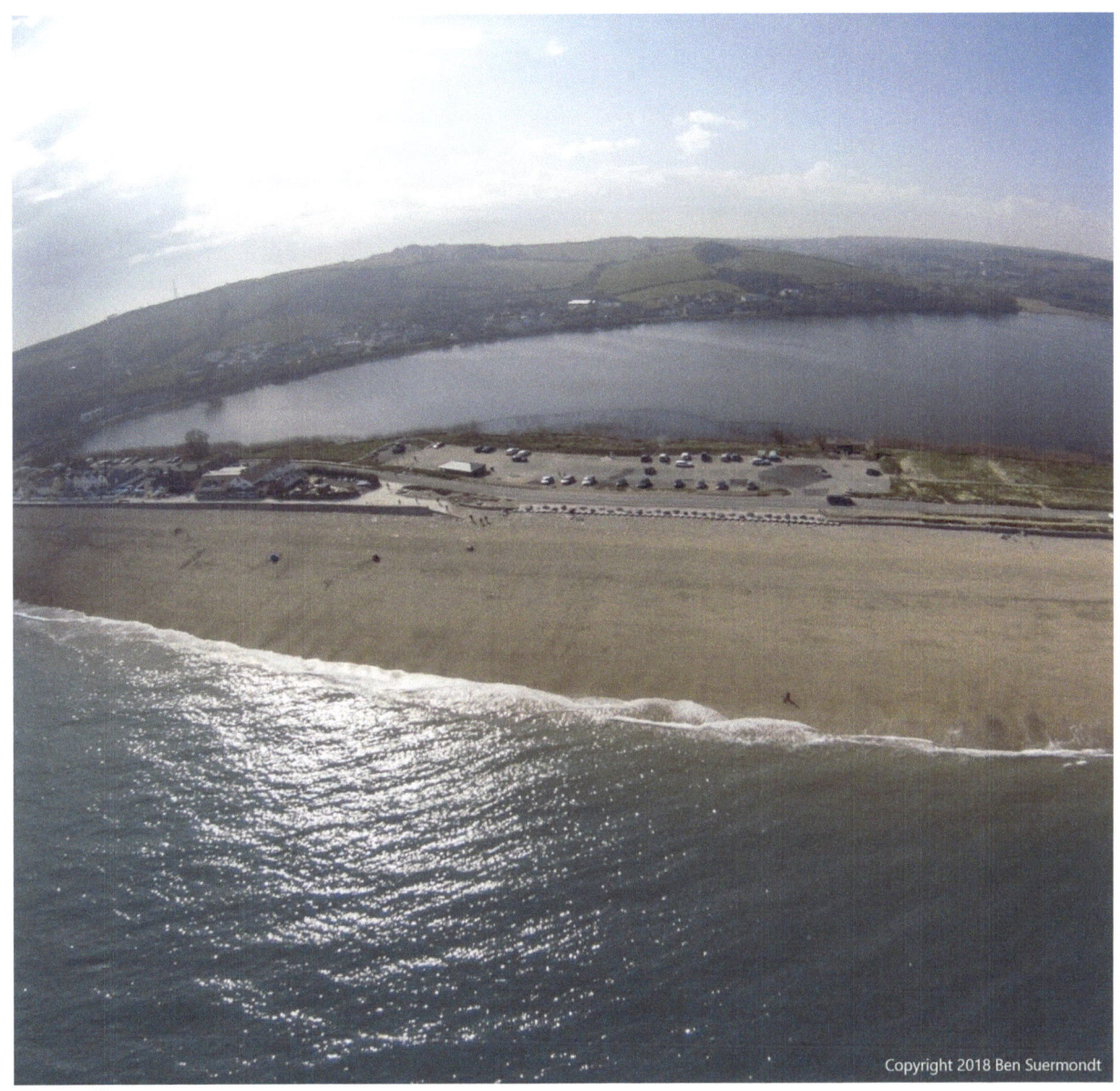

Above: Torcross

Thank you for sharing your time and enjoying these breath taking views I captured using a drone only.

www.ingramcontent.com/pod-product-compliance
Lightning Source LLC
Chambersburg PA
CBHW040057250526
45473CB00043B/1810